J.S. BACH

T0081654

2 Air on the G String

6 Aria

14 Be Thou with Me (Bist du bei mir)

11 Gavotte

18 Jesu, Joy of Man's Desiring

23 Largo

28 March

34 Minuet in G

38 Musette

31 Sheep May Safely Graze

46 Siciliano

42 Sleepers, Awake (Wachet auf)

ISBN 978-1-4950-4511-0

HAL•LEONARD® CORPORATION

7777 W. Bluemound Rd. P.O. Box 13819 Milwaukee, WI 53213

In Australia Contact:
Hal Leonard Australia Pty. Ltd.
4 Lentara Court
Cheltenham, Victoria, 3192 Australia
Email: ausadmin@halleonard.com.au

For all works contained herein:
Unauthorized copying, arranging, adapting, recording, Internet posting, public performance, or other distribution of the printed music in this publication is an infringement of copyright. Infringers are liable under the law.

Visit Hal Leonard Online at
www.halleonard.com

AIR ON THE G STRING

from ORCHESTRAL SUITE NO. 3

By JOHANN SEBASTIAN BACH

Copyright © 2015 by HAL LEONARD CORPORATION
International Copyright Secured All Rights Reserved

1.
2.

3
pp

ARIA
from THE GOLDBERG VARIATIONS

By JOHANN SEBASTIAN BACH

Copyright © 2015 by HAL LEONARD CORPORATION
International Copyright Secured All Rights Reserved

3

Moderately fast Swing
mf

A tempo

GAVOTTE
from FRENCH SUITE NO. 5

By JOHANN SEBASTIAN BACH

Copyright © 2015 by HAL LEONARD CORPORATION
International Copyright Secured All Rights Reserved

To Coda
Hard Swing

3

3
3

1.
2.
Straight 8ths
D.S. al Coda
CODA
molto rit.
pp
8vb

BE THOU WITH ME

(Bist du bei mir)

By JOHANN SEBASTIAN BACH

Copyright © 2015 by HAL LEONARD CORPORATION
International Copyright Secured All Rights Reserved

Straight 8ths

Straight 8ths
Straight 8ths

3
3
3
Straight 8ths
3
Slower
rit.

JESU, JOY OF MAN'S DESIRING

By JOHANN SEBASTIAN BACH

Copyright © 2015 by HAL LEONARD CORPORATION
International Copyright Secured All Rights Reserved

rit.

LARGO

from Piano Concerto in F minor

By JOHANN SEBASTIAN BACH

Copyright © 2015 by HAL LEONARD CORPORATION
International Copyright Secured All Rights Reserved

A tempo

MARCH
from THE ANNA MAGDALENA NOTEBOOK

By JOHANN SEBASTIAN BACH

Copyright © 2015 by HAL LEONARD CORPORATION
International Copyright Secured All Rights Reserved

2.
To Coda

D.S. al Coda
CODA

SHEEP MAY SAFELY GRAZE

from CANTATA NO. 208

By JOHANN SEBASTIAN BACH

Copyright © 2015 by HAL LEONARD CORPORATION
International Copyright Secured All Rights Reserved

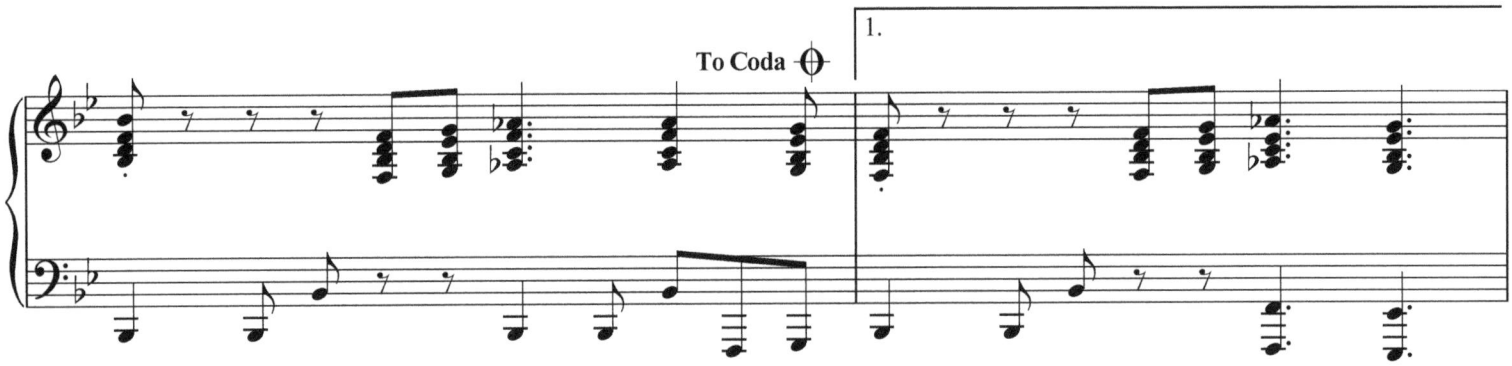
To Coda
1.

2.

D.S. al Coda
CODA
molto rit.
8vb

MINUET IN G
from THE ANNA MAGDALENA NOTEBOOK

By JOHANN SEBASTIAN BACH

Copyright © 2015 by HAL LEONARD CORPORATION
International Copyright Secured All Rights Reserved

1.
2.
1
4
1
To Coda

1.
2.

D.C. al Coda
CODA
rit.

MUSETTE
from THE ANNA MAGDALENA NOTEBOOK

By JOHANN SEBASTIAN BACH

Copyright © 2015 by HAL LEONARD CORPORATION
International Copyright Secured All Rights Reserved

To Coda

D.S. al Coda

CODA

SLEEPERS WAKE
(Wachet auf)

By JOHANN SEBASTIAN BACH

Copyright © 2015 by HAL LEONARD CORPORATION
International Copyright Secured All Rights Reserved

3
1.
2.
f

mp
p
molto rall.
pp

SICILIANO

By JOHANN SEBASTIAN BACH

Copyright © 2015 by HAL LEONARD CORPORATION
International Copyright Secured All Rights Reserved

Straight 8ths